D0989765

Family Photographs

JOAN ALBERT

Mine

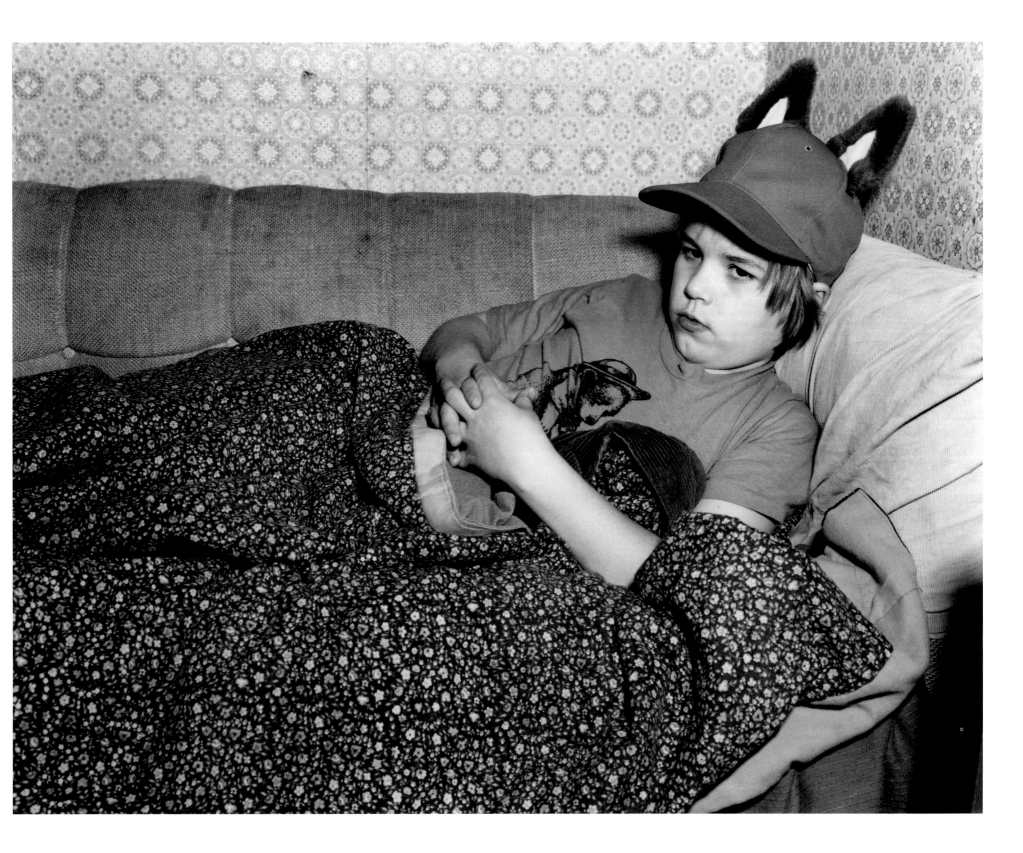

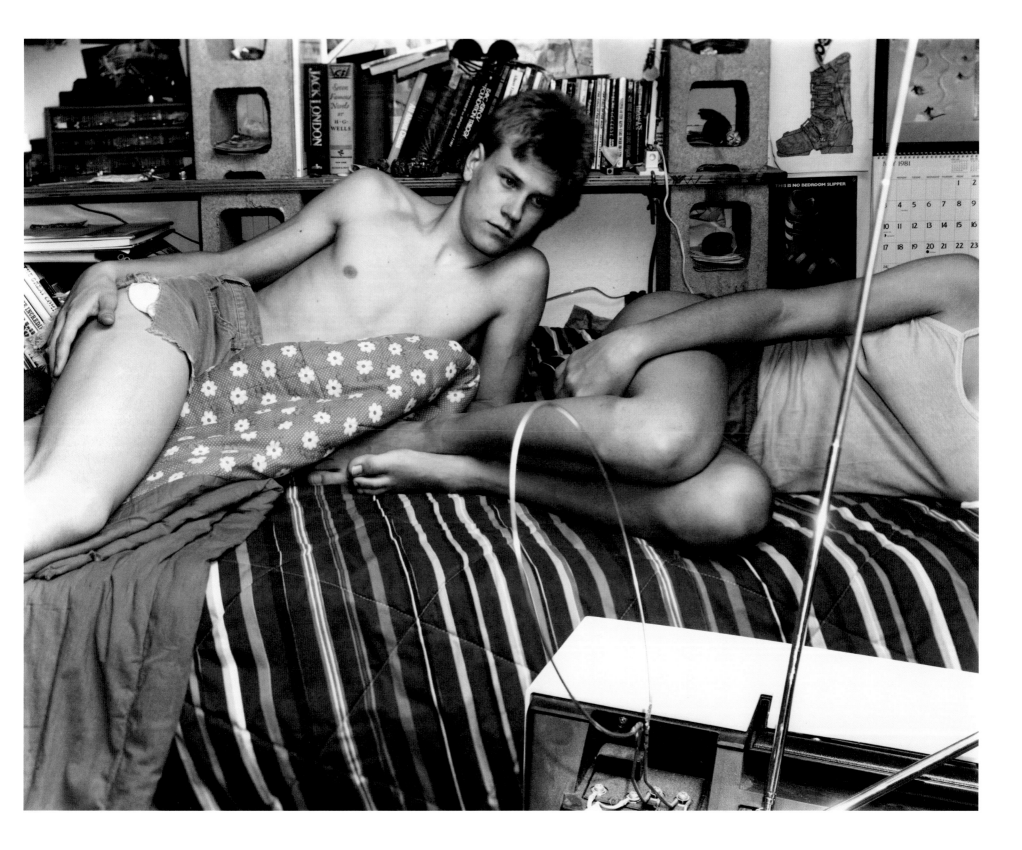

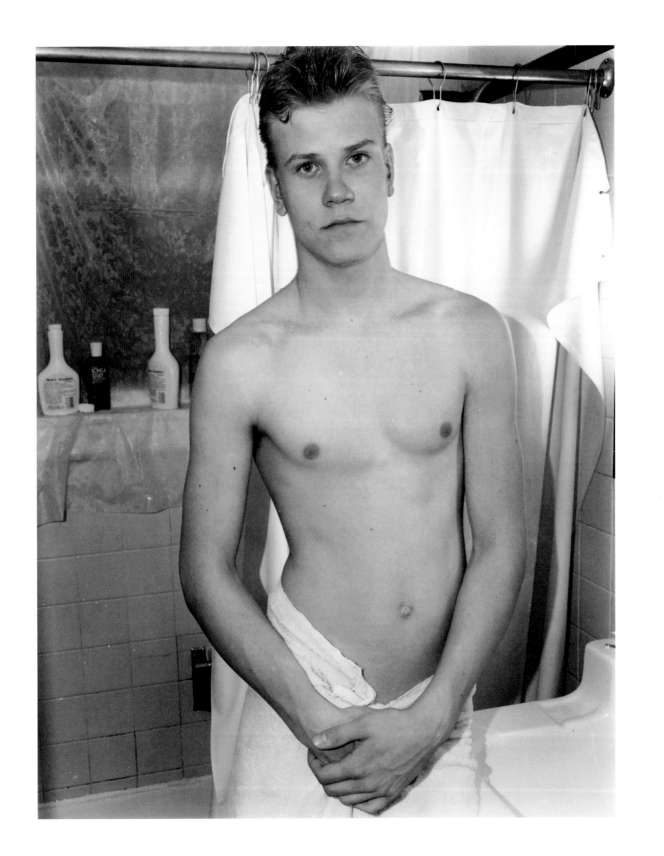

33

MINE

1. Martin in bed
Cambridge, MA
1978

2. Nathan at nine
Cambridge, MA
1980

3. Martin
Cambridge, MA
1978

4. Nathan
Cambridge, MA
October 1980

5. Martin at fifteen
Cambridge, MA
October 1980

6. Dad
Deerfield, NH
Circa 1980

7. Martin & Kyra
Cambridge, MA
1981

8. Nathan
Cambridge, MA
1981

9. Martin & Nathan
Cambridge, MA
1980

10. Nathan & Martin
Cambridge, MA
1979

11. Martin
Cambridge, MA
1981

12. Nathan in bed
Cambridge, MA
1980

13. Martin
Cambridge, MA
May 1981

14. Nathan
Cambridge, MA
1982

15. Martin at fifteen
Cambridge, MA
April 1981

16. Martin & Kyra
Cambridge, MA
1983

17. Dad & Mom
Watertown, MA
1981

18. Martin at nineteen
Cambridge, MA
July 1984

19. Nathan in his room
Cambridge, MA
1982

20. Dad
Monmouth, ME
January 1987

21. Martin in his room
Cambridge, MA
June 1982

22. Nathan
Cambridge, MA
1981

23. Martin & Kyra
Cambridge, MA
1981

24. Mom & Dad
Cambridge, MA
Circa 1991

25. Martin
Cambridge, MA
July 1983

26. Nathan
Cambridge, MA
October 1983

27. Martin at nineteen
Cambridge, MA
January 1985

28. Martin at twenty
Cambridge, MA
May 1985

29. Nathan & Martin
Cambridge, MA
January 1988

30. Nathan in his bedroom
Cambridge, MA
1988

31. Emily & Nathan
Cambridge, MA
1989

32. Martin
Cambridge, MA
1984

33. Dad & Mom
Watertown, MA
1989

34. Dad
Watertown, MA
March 1989

35. Martin
Cambridge, MA
October 1984

Theirs

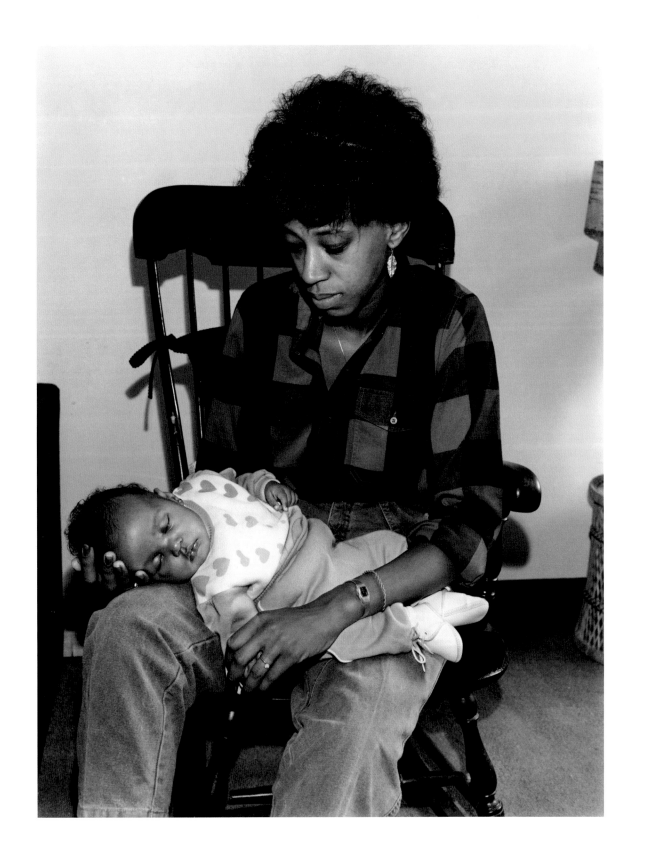

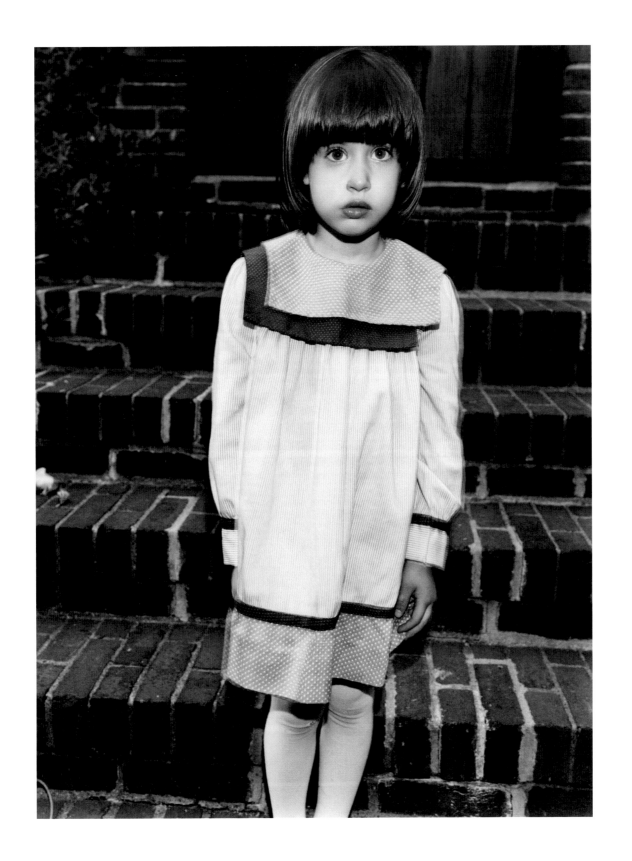

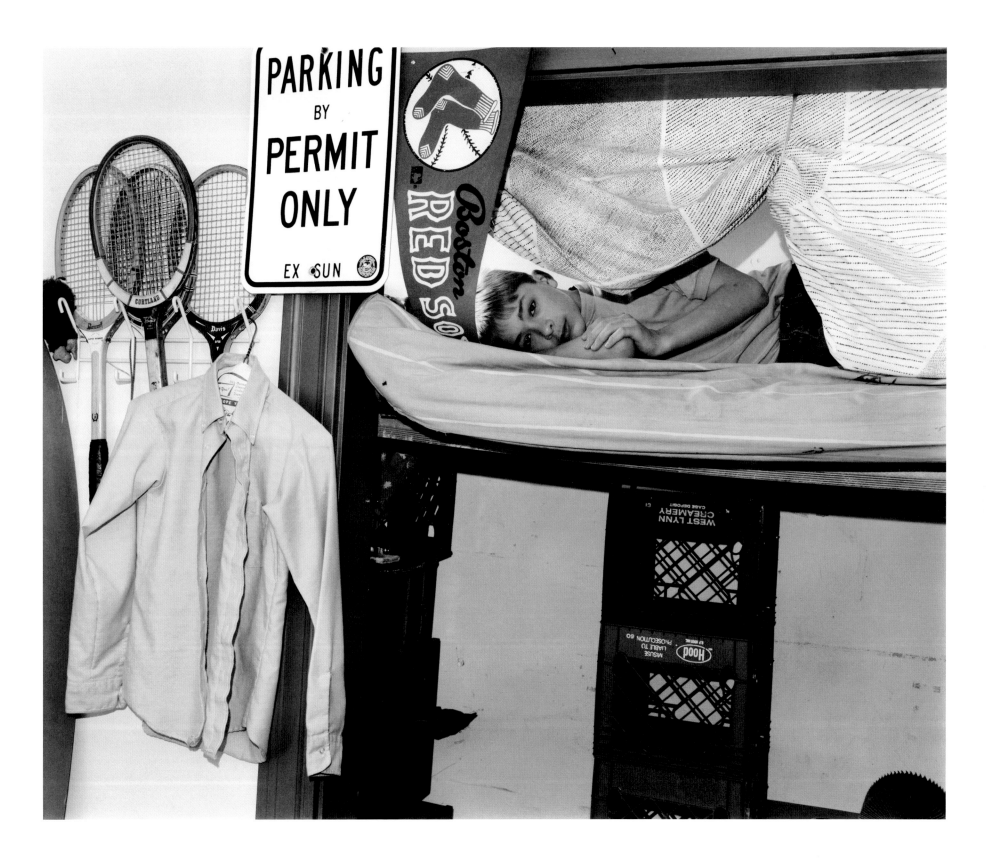

THEIRS

36. Becky & Neville
New Hampshire
Circa 1988

37. Chrissy holding Erin
Cambridge, MA
March 1982

38. Esther & grandchild
Cambridge, MA
December 1984

39. Mimi & Alexander
MA
May 1983

40. Father & sons
Worcester, MA
December 1985

41. Sally's son
MA
May 1983

42. Mother & daughters
Somerville, MA
May 1983

43. Donny & Mia
MA
January 1983

44. Miguel & Adrienne
Cambridge, MA
Circa 1982

45. Miguel & Adrienne
Cambridge, MA
Circa 1984

46. Siblings
MA
Circa 1980

47. Sisters in car
MA
1980

48. Girl on steps
MA
Circa 1982

49. Girl
Wakefield, MA
April 1982

50. Mother & child
MA
Circa 1981

51. Penny & Lisa
MA
January 1982

52. Mother & daughters
Newton, MA
1982

53. Becca (niece)
Denver, CO
1987

54. Walker
Cambridge, MA
February 1983

55. Peggy & Walker
Cambridge, MA
November 1983

56. Debbie & Rachel
MA
Circa 1981

57. Brother & sister
Somerville, MA
October 1985

58. Debbie & Rachel
Cambridge, MA
Febuary 1985

59. Shayla & Brendon
Cambridge, MA
June 1983

60. Dorothea & Luis
MA
December 1984

61. Robin & Ben
MA
May 1984

62. Amy (niece)
Denver, CO
August 1987

JOAN ALBERT (1943-2012)

Joan Albert created a remarkable body of work over a short period of time from the 1970s through the early 1990s. Her intimate photographs of her growing sons are filled with emotion, humor, and the obsessions of teenage and pre-teenage boys of that era. Her portraits of friends and neighbors with their children are similarly poignant and richly detailed, showing the complexity and intensity of parent-child relationships.

I first met Joan in 1979, when I sat in on a class of Nick Nixon's at the Massachusetts College of Art, where Joan was getting her MFA. Joan was in her mid-30s, and was raising two sons on her own. Her middle son, Jason, had died in an accident, and — between her experience of motherhood and of loss — she seemed infinitely older and wiser than me, someone I could learn from about life as well as photography. She loved her children more than anything, and she loved the ability of the 4x5" view camera to beautifully render and preserve moments of their rapidly changing lives. She was also eager to capture the subtleties of parent-child dynamics in other families, and photographed and re-photographed her friends, neighbors, and strangers with great delicacy and empathy. As a friend, she was thoughtful, vivacious, and incredibly funny. We would sit in her kitchen, talking, laughing, and looking at each other's pictures, while her sons' lives whirled around us.

Joan taught photography at Massachusetts College of Art for a number of years, and eventually went back to school to get a social work degree so that she would be more empowered to help others. In 1987, it was discovered that she had a benign tumor on her spine, and she endured multiple surgeries and lived much of the rest of her life with chronic pain and disability. It soon became physically impossible for her to continue photographing, so she turned to writing essays and short stories, and to enjoying watching her sons turn into young men with families of their own. She endured her life's many hardships with courage, grace, and always a sense of humor.

Joan exhibited her work widely, and her photographs are in the collections of the Museum of Modern Art, NY, the Fogg Museum at Harvard University, and the Polaroid Collection at MIT in Cambridge, MA.

Sage Sohier
Boston, MA
2021

ACKNOWLEDGEMENTS

This book was made possible through the generous support of the following individuals:

Martin Albert

Nathan Albert

Stephen Albert

Karl Baden

Michael Foley

Gregory Jundanian

Mary Anne Karia

Susan and Chris Lane

Phyllis Menken

Mike Mikulka

Steve Mikulka

Wendy Morgan

Nancy Myerson

Nick and Bebe Nixon

Phyllis and Ken Nobel

Chris Rauschenberg

Kent Rodzwicz

Irina Rozovsky

Sheron Rupp

Joel Shield

Sage Sohier

Mark Steinmetz

Barbara Wachter

Chris Wilkinson

Toby Yarmolinsky

Published by STANLEY/BARKER
First Edition 2022

ISBN 978-1-913288-38-9   S/B067A

Images © Albert Estate
Edition © STANLEY/BARKER

Edited by Sage Sohier
Lettering & End Pages by Tamara Shopsin
Scans by Kent Rodzwicz
Printed By EBS, EU